For the Teacher

This reproducible study guide consists of lessons to use in conjunction with a specific novel. Used together, the books and the guide provide an exciting supplement to the basal reader in your classroom. Written in chapter-by-chapter format, the guide contains a synopsis, pre-reading activities, vocabulary and comprehension exercises, as well as extension activities to be used as follow-up to the novel.

In a homogeneous classroom, whole class instruction with one title is appropriate. In a heterogeneous classroom, reading groups should be formed: each group works on a different novel on its reading level. Depending upon the length of time devoted to reading in the classroom, each novel, with its guide and accompanying lessons, may be completed in three to six weeks.

Begin using NOVEL-TIES for reading development by distributing the novel and a folder to each child. Distribute duplicated pages of the study guide for students to place in their folders. After examining the cover and glancing through the book, students can participate in several pre-reading activities. Vocabulary questions should be considered before reading the book. Comprehension questions can be answered orally or in writing. The classroom teacher should determine the amount of work to be assigned, always keeping in mind that readers must be nurtured and that the ultimate goal is encouraging students' love of reading.

The benefits of using NOVEL-TIES are numerous. Students read good literature in the original, rather than in abridged or edited form. The good reading habits, formed by practice in focusing on interpretive comprehension and literary techniques, will be transferred to the books students read independently. Passive readers become active, avid readers.

Novel-Ties are printed on recycled paper.

SYNOPSIS

Based on the real-life experiences of the author's family, this is the story of a Japanese family's escape from northern Korea to Japan at the end of World War II. As the war draws to a close and the defeat of Japan is imminent, the Japanese who are living in Korea are suddenly in grave danger. They are bitterly resented by the Koreans because their country has been under Japanese control for many years.

On July 29, 1945, alerted by a family friend that she and her family are being sought by the Korean Communists, Mrs. Kawashima and her two daughters – Ko, age 16, and Yoko, age 11 – flee the family's comfortable home in a bamboo grove. She leaves behind messages for Mr. Kawashima and Hideyo, her eighteen-year-old son, who are away from home at the time.

The women board a Japanese medical train that is heading to Seoul, in southern Korea. Korean Communists board the boxcar in search of the Kawashimas, but the medics disguise them as patients, and do not reveal their identities. About forty-five miles from Seoul, the train is hit and disabled by enemy aircraft, causing the Kawashima women to set out on foot for the remainder of the journey.

As the women proceed south, they are confronted by three Korean Communist soldiers with machine guns. Suddenly, an airplane flies overhead and the women throw themselves to the ground. The three soldiers are killed by the shelling from the plane, but the women survive. Yoko's right ear and chest, however, are wounded.

Arriving in Seoul, the Kawashima women seek medical care for Yoko's injuries at the Japanese hospital tent. Yoko recovers, but loses her hearing in one ear. When the conditions become too dangerous for them to remain in Seoul, the women leave by boat for Japan with many other refugees.

Meanwhile, the factory where Hideyo is working is taken over by Korean Communist soldiers. He manages to escape, and returns home to find a note from his mother telling him that she will meet him in Seoul at the train station. During his long journey on foot to Seoul, he must hide from a roving band of Korean Communist soldiers.

Weak from exhaustion, Hideyo collapses on the doorstep of a Korean family. They nurse him back to health.

After their arrival in Japan, the women live for a month in a refugee camp. In November, Yoko, along with her mother and sister, set out by train for northern Japan to find her grandparents. Mrs. Kawashima suddenly decides to get off the train at Kyoto, because she knows that the city has escaped massive bombing, and she wants her daughters to continue their schooling. After enrolling the girls at school, she resumes her trip north.

When Mother returns to Kyoto, she meets Yoko at the train station, and reports to her that all of their relatives have perished in the war. She then dies in Yoko's arms. Ko arrives at the station soon afterwards, and the girls accompany their mother's body to a crematorium. Mrs. Masuda, a compassionate stranger, offers the girls lodging in her warehouse.

Ko and Yoko continue to attend school and live in the warehouse throughout the winter, subsisting on a meager diet, and making periodic trips to the port city of Maizuru to look for Hideyo. Each time they go to Maizuru, they post a sign with their address, hoping he is looking for them.

In the spring, Hideyo decides that he must leave the farmhouse of the Korean family where he has been hiding. He makes a daring escape across the 38th parallel to southern Korea, and sets out to find his family in Japan. Arriving at Maizuru in Japan, Hideyo finds Yoko's sign near the harbor. Yoko, Ko, and Hideyo are soon joyously reunited in Kyoto.

PRE-READING ACTIVITIES

1. Locate Korea on a world map. Then look at the map of Korea at the beginning of the book. Find the 38th parallel which divides Communist North Korea from South Korea. Locate Nanam, the town in North Korea where the Kawashima family lives when the story opens. As you read the story, use the map to help you trace the family's journey. Also locate Manchuria, a part of China, and the Russian port cities of Vladivostok and Nakhodka. Notice their proximity to North Korea.

2. Read the publisher's notes at the end of the book and do some additional research on the history of Korea. Learn about its relationship with Japan. Why did the Koreans have grievances against the Japanese? As you read the book, continue to refer to the publisher's notes to gain a historical perspective on the story as it unfolds.

3. This novel will help you gain a better understanding of what life is like for civilians in a war-torn country. Before you begin to read, collect some newspaper and magazine articles which describe the effects of war or violent conflict on a civilian population. Share your findings with your classmates.

4. If you had to leave home suddenly, taking with you only what you could carry in a backpack, what items would you take with you? Make a list containing items you would need for survival, as well as some special items with personal meaning for you.

5. Yoko, the main character in this novel, must enroll in a new school in a new city when she arrives in Japan. Have you ever had to change to a new school? What are some fears or worries you had before you made the change?

6. Read the author's dedication at the beginning of the book. What role do you think Catherine Woolley played in Yoko Kawashima Watkin's life?

7. Find some examples of calligraphy, or Chinese brush writing. Try to determine why this form of writing is considered a fine art in China. Then do some research to learn about the role of calligraphy in Imperial China and its importance in modern China.

CHAPTER 1

Vocabulary: Draw a line from each word on the left to its definition on the right. Then use the numbered words to fill in the blanks in the sentences below.

1. frolic
2. bewildered
3. emphatic
4. insecure
5. demolished
6. disfigured
7. vermilion
8. tributary

a. unsafe
b. stream feeding a larger stream or river
c. vivid red color
d. play happily
e. forceful in speech
f. confused
g. destroyed
h. defaced by injuries

. . . .

1. To prevent highway accidents, you must be _____ when you teach the rules of the road.

2. All of the residents were upset when they learned that their building would be _____ to make room for a new road.

3. We smiled happily as we watched the children _____ in the park on a warm spring afternoon.

4. I was so _____ by the directions to the game that I put it away and never tried to play it again.

5. Without the protection of her older sister, the child felt _____.

6. My brother was so badly _____ in the auto accident, I did not recognize him when I went to the hospital.

7. The woman's fingernails were painted an eye-catching shade of _____.

8. The swiftly-flowing current of the _____ carried the boats to the river.

Questions:

1. Why are Mother and her daughters planning to leave Korea as the story begins?

2. What precautions has Yoko's family taken against the dangers of war?

3. How does Yoko react when the Japanese army police come to her? What do her actions reveal about her character?

Chapter 1 (cont.)

4. What news does Mr. Enomoto give his students? Why isn't Yoko as upset as some of her classmates?

5. Why does Corporal Matsumura feel grateful to Yoko's family? How does their relationship with him prove to be helpful to the family?

6. How do Yoko's parents feel about Japan's war policies?

7. What important decision does Hideyo make? How does Ko try to convince her brother not to do this? How effective is her plea?

8. Why must the three women flee to the train station?

Questions for Discussion:

1. Why do you think Japanese soldiers treated Mother, Yoko, and Ko so brutally?

2. Why do you think Yoko's parents make sure their children's education continues during wartime, particularly emphasizing calligraphy and the tea ceremony?

3. Do you think Mother should have waited for Hideyo's return before leaving? How do you think she and her daughters will manage on their own?

Literary Devices:

I. *Simile* — A simile is a figure of speech in which two unlike objects are compared using the words "like" or "as." For example:

So tiny, this hand. Like a miniature maple leaf.

What is Corporal Matsumura comparing?

_____

What is the effect of this comparison?

_____

_____

Complete each of the following phrases with a simile of your own.

1. The air raid siren was as loud as _____

_____

2. The shovel which Yoko used to dig ditches was as heavy as _____

_____

3. Yoko danced as gracefully as a _____

_____

Chapter 1 (cont.)

4. The cracking of the bamboo was like the sound of _____

_____

5. Corporal Matsumura's scarred face in the candlelight was as frightening as

_____

II. *Point of View* — Point of view in literature refers to the voice telling the story. It could be one of the characters or the author narrating the story. From whose point of view is this story told?

_____

Why do you think the author chose this point of view?

_____

Writing Activity:

1. Pretend that you are Hideyo and write a letter to Father in which you express your reasons for wanting to join Japan's Imperial Army.
2. Pretend you are Yoko and write a journal entry expressing your thoughts and feelings as you leave Korea.

CHAPTER 2

Vocabulary: Use the context to help you figure out the meaning of the underlined word in each of the following sentences. Then compare your definition with a dictionary definition.

1. As I hurried away from the accident, my stomach was churning with fright.

    Your definition _____

    Dictionary definition _____

2. A vigorous officer was shouting and directing traffic.

    Your definition _____

    Dictionary definition _____

3. Once the dark enveloped the train, I could not see the scenes flying by outside.

    Your definition _____

    Dictionary definition _____

4. After the train was bombed, the medics began to evacuate the patients to the hospital.

    Your definition _____

    Dictionary definition _____

5. Despite the continued bombing, everyone on the train gallantly began to help the medics carry the patients to safety.

    Your definition _____

    Dictionary definition _____

6. For fear that someone would betray us, Mother warned us to keep our plans a secret.

    Your definition _____

    Dictionary definition _____

7. There was such a commotion on the railroad platform that we could not find the station master or hear the announcements.

    Your definition _____

    Dictionary definition _____

Chapter 2 (cont.)

Questions:

1. Who are the soldiers that Mother, Yoko, and Ko almost encounter on their flight from home? What are they practicing?
2. Why is the Kawashima family allowed to board the medical train that is heading to Seoul, even though they are not patients?
3. Describe the conditions in the boxcar in which Yoko and her family travel.
4. Why won't Mother let Yoko eat any of the food in her sack while they are in the boxcar? Do you think she is right?
5. Why do the medics throw the dead bodies from the train? Do you think they are cruel to do so?
6. Why do Korean Communist soldiers board the train?
7. Why does Mother decide that she and her daughters should leave the train and walk to Seoul?

Questions for Discussion:

1. Do you think Mother and Ko are too hard on Yoko as they escape from their home?
2. How do you think you would have behaved if you were in Yoko's place on the train?
3. How do you think the Korean soldiers learn that there are healthy people on board the train?

Literary Device: Sensory Details

An author often uses *sensory details* to describe the setting of a novel. Re-read the passage in which Yoko describes her first impressions of the boxcar. Locate the words that evoke each of the senses below:

1. SIGHT _____
2. SMELL _____
3. SOUND _____
4. TOUCH _____

Writing Activity:

Imagine you are a reporter and write about the scene you witness when the hospital train to Seoul is bombed. Describe what happens to the train and the passengers on board.

CHAPTERS 3, 4

Vocabulary: Synonyms are words with similar meanings. Draw a line from each word in column A to its synonym in column B. Then use the words in column A to fill in the blanks in the sentences below.

A	B
1. torrents	a. reflexively
2. yearned	b. furtively
3. automatically	c. threatening
4. munitions	d. craved
5. stealthily	e. stink
6. desolation	f. floods
7. ominous	g. ruin
8. stench	h. weapons

· ·

1. The frequent bombing caused _____ throughout the city.

2. A well-trained Seeing Eye dog _____ stops in its tracks at a curb or flight of stairs.

3. The hungry child _____ for something to fill his stomach.

4. The factory where my brother works produces _____ for the war.

5. We crept _____ through the woods to avoid being captured by enemy troops.

6. The _____ of the spilled garbage permeated the house.

7. We gazed down fearfully at the swirling _____ of water below the bridge.

8. The _____ sound of the thunder warned us of an approaching storm.

Questions:

1. As they begin their journey on foot to Seoul, what precautions do the Kawashima women take to avoid capture by the Korean Communists?

2. How does Ko show her resourcefulness on the journey to Seoul?

3. Why are Yoko, Ko, and Mother able to survive the airplane attack?

Chapters 3, 4 (cont.)

4. How do the women disguise themselves as they continue on their journey to Seoul? Why does Mother shave the girls' heads?

5. How does Hideyo avoid being killed by the Communist soldiers who capture the factory?

6. Why is Hideyo able to find Mother's note, even though the house has been ransacked by the troops?

7. Why are there Korean refugees as well as Japanese like Hideyo walking along the rails to Seoul?

Questions for Discussion:

1. Do you think Yoko acts like a spoiled child on the journey to Seoul? Why is she uncooperative at times?

2. Do you think Ko is unnecessarily bossy on the journey? Might Yoko and her mother have survived without Ko?

3. Why do you think Hideyo and his companions are able to trick the Russian soldiers into believing they are Korean orphans?

Literary Device: Point of View

From whose point of view is Chapter Four written?

_____

Why do you think the author changed the point of view?

_____

_____

Writing Activity:

Imagine that your life is in danger and, like Hideyo, you only have a few minutes before you must leave your home. Tell what you would do in the short time that is available to you.

CHAPTER 5

Vocabulary: Use the words in the Word Box and the clues below to complete the crossword puzzle.

> **WORD BOX**
>
> altercation   alumni   feeble   cunning
> dehydrate   spunky   stout
> asylum   peril   interrogation   confine

Across

2. remove water from
6. act of questioning
7. graduates of a particular school or institution
8. fat, portly
9. physically weak
11. spirited, plucky

Down

1. danger, jeopardy
3. heated or angry dispute
4. shrewdness, slyness
5. enclose within bounds
10. refuge, sanctuary

Chapter 5 (cont.)

Questions:

1. Why does Ko say to Yoko, "This journey would be easier if you had got killed"? Do you think she really means this? Why or why not?

2. Why do people mistake Mother, Ko, and Yoko for Koreans?

3. Why does Mother drop suddenly to the ground in a faint at the interrogation checkpoint?

4. What evidence shows that Yoko has been very brave since she received her wound?

5. Why does Mother insist on staying in Seoul after she has been warned to leave? Why does Ko insist that she and her mother and sister must leave Seoul?

6. How do Ko and Yoko leave word for Hideyo to let him know they are taking the freight train to Pusan?

7. How does Ko manage to smuggle the family's precious sword onto the boat when they leave for Japan?

Questions for Discussion:

1. How has the difficult journey changed Mother, Ko, and Yoko? How do you think you might survive such a journey?

2. Why do you think Ko and Mother cry as they leave Korea for Japan?

Social Studies / Math Connection:

Use the map at the front of the book with its scale of miles to determine approximately how far Yoko and her family walked from Nanam to Seoul.

Writing Activity:

Write about someone you know or someone you have read abut who is sufficiently brave and resourceful to be a good companion on a difficult journey. Tell why you would want to be with this person in times of danger.

CHAPTERS 6, 7

Vocabulary: Use the context to help you figure out the meaning of the underlined word in each of the following sentences. Then compare your definition with a dictionary definition.

1. After ransacking all of the houses in town, the soldiers stuffed their bags full of <u>plunder</u> and left quickly.

   Your definition   _____

   Dictionary definition   _____

2. When those who were near me heard my cough, they scattered, as if I were carrying <u>contagion</u>.

   Your definition   _____

   Dictionary definition   _____

3. The few belongings we have in our knapsack are the only <u>mementos</u> from our beloved home.

   Your definition   _____

   Dictionary definition   _____

4. After traveling for three days and nights without food or water, we felt we could <u>endure</u> anything.

   Your definition   _____

   Dictionary definition   _____

5. As soon as we saw a <u>vacancy</u> on the bench, we pushed our way forward and sat down.

   Your definition   _____

   Dictionary definition   _____

6. After experiencing the hardships of war, I was <u>compassionate</u> toward others who experienced the same.

   Your definition   _____

   Dictionary definition   _____

Chapters 6, 7 (cont.)

Questions:

1. Why does Hideyo avoid walking on the railroad tracks on his journey to Seoul?
2. What evidence of brutality does Hideyo witness as he tries to hide from Korean Communist soldiers?
3. How does Hideyo – alone, starving, and almost frozen – give himself the courage to continue on his journey?
4. Why is Yoko disappointed when she arrives in Fukuoka, Japan?
5. Why does Mother decide to leave the train in Kyoto instead of going to her home town of Aomori?
6. How does Mother reply when Yoko complains that she has no clothes to wear to school?
7. How do Yoko's refugee experiences prepare her for the first day of school in Kyoto?

Questions for Discussion:

1. Whose southward journey do you think was more difficult – that of Hideyo or Mother with Yoko and Ko?
2. How do you think Mother, Ko, and Yoko's arrival in Japan differed from what they expected?
3. Do you think Mother was right to leave Yoko at school so soon after they arrived in Kyoto?
4. What might school officials have done to make Yoko's first day easier?

Writing Activity:

Write about a time when you or someone you know was teased. Tell why the teasing occurred and how the victim reacted.

CHAPTER 8

Vocabulary: Draw a line from each word on the left to its definition on the right. Then use the numbered words to fill in the blanks in the sentences below.

1. prestigious
2. anguish
3. crematorium
4. urn
5. tatami

a. straw floor mats
b. ornamental vase
c. extreme distress
d. honored
e. building where the bodies of the dead are burned

. . . .

1. In a Japanese home, _____ cover the floors of each room.

2. The young woman suffered great _____ when she learned of the death of her friend.

3. In accordance with her will, we brought Grandmother's body to a(n) _____ after her death.

4. Grandmother's ashes were placed in a large _____.

5. Many students compete to attend a(n) _____ college.

Questions:

1. Why does Yoko befriend the trash man at school?

2. Why does the trash man rip up the drawing of Yoko which her classmates hang in the classroom?

3. Why does Yoko suddenly begin to feel protective of Mother in the train station?

4. After her mother dies, why does Yoko say, "I made up my mind I would never step into a Buddhist temple as long as I lived"?

5. How do Ko and Yoko honor their mother's memory in their new home?

Questions for Discussion:

1. Why do you think the education of her children was so important to Mother? Is education very important to your family? Give examples to support your statements.

2. Why do you think Mrs. Masuda helped Yoko and Ko with their mother's funeral arrangements and accompanied them to the crematorium?

Chapter 8 (cont.)

Literary Device: Personification

Personification is a literary device in which an author grants human qualities to an inanimate object. For example:

> All the way to the station my heart was skipping and hopping
> with happiness.

What is personified?

_____

What is the effect of this device?

_____

_____

Writing Activity:

Write an editorial for a newspaper in Kyoto in which you speak out against the inhumane actions of the people who were unkind to Ko and Yoko after Mother's death, and praise the actions of the people who showed compassion to them. Be sure to close with a strong statement of your opinion.

CHAPTER 9

Vocabulary: Analogies are equations in which the first pair of words has the same relationship as the second pair of words. For example: CONCLUDE is to COMMENCE as DAWN is to DUSK. Both pairs of words are opposites. Choose a word from the Word Box to complete each of the analogies below.

```
                    WORD BOX
        vicinity              staggered
        negotiating           humble
        reverently            earnestly
```

1. HONESTLY is to CANDIDLY as SERIOUSLY is to _____.

2. SEWING is to QUILT as _____ is to TREATY.

3. PROUD is to STRUTTED as EXHAUSTED is to _____.

4. BEG is to PLEAD as LOCALE is to _____.

5. ARROGANT is to _____ as GRACEFUL is to AWKWARD.

6. RESPECTFULLY is to _____ as HASTILY is to RAPIDLY.

Questions:

1. Why does Yoko say to Ko, "Mother's last words haunt me"? How does Yoko's persistence to find out the meaning of Mother's words pay off?
2. Why do the sisters travel to Maizuru?
3. What secret does Yoko discover about Ko on New Year's Eve? Why does she spend her shoe money after learning this secret?
4. Why is the girls' New Year's Eve celebration also a birthday celebration?
5. How would you now characterize Yoko and Ko's relationship? How has it changed?

Chapter 9 (cont.)

Literary Device: Metaphor

A metaphor is a figure of speech in which there is an implied comparison: For example:

> I will beat every one of them with my grades. The grades are the only weapon I have now.

What is being compared?

_____

What does Yoko mean?

_____

_____

Writing Activity:

Despite their humiliating circumstances, the terrible shock of Mother's death, and their concern for Hideyo and Father, Yoko and Ko are able to celebrate New Year's Eve by buying each other special treats for their meal together. Why do you think they are both so "overwhelmed" by their humble meal? Can you think of a time when you have been deeply moved by a simple, but special, gift from another person? Write a first-person account of your experience.

CHAPTER 10

Vocabulary: Draw a line from each word on the left to its definition on the right.
Then use the numbered words to fill in the blanks in the sentences below.

1. numb
2. snobbish
3. suspension
4. spared
5. prohibited
6. textile
7. wracked

a. unharmed
b. forbidden
c. strained or afflicted
d. lacking sensation
e. woven or knit cloth
f. temporary removal
g. possessing an offensive air of superiority

. . . .

1. The child's small body was _____ by sobs when her mother left.

2. The _____ factory manufactures a variety of fabrics.

3. The airplane crash took the lives of most of the passengers, although a few were _____ .

4. The _____ behavior of the other girls made me feel worthless.

5. My fingers and toes became _____ from the penetrating cold.

6. The girl's _____ from school occurred after she broke the rules many times.

7. With concern for their workers' health, the factory owners _____ smoking in the building.

Questions:

1. How does Ko amaze the classmates who tease her at the university?

2. Why is winter particularly hard for Yoko and Ko?

3. How does the title of Yoko's essay, "Understanding," express the opposite of what is true? What does Yoko do with her prize money?

4. Yoko says, "Not a single teacher mentioned the prize. Obviously the school was not pleased." Why was the school displeased with Yoko's winning essay?

5. Why does Yoko conceal the fact of her mother's death from the school authorities?

6. Why does Yoko have such a strong emotional reaction when she sees Corporal Matsumura?

Chapter 10 (cont.)

Questions for Discussion:

1. What did you learn about the behavior that was expected of young Japanese single women in the 1940s?

2. Why do you think Corporal Matsumura feels a continuing attachment to Yoko? Do you think he did enough to help her and her sister?

3. Why do you think the principal seems indifferent to Yoko's problems?

4. Why do you think Hideyo has not yet arrived in Japan?

Writing Activity:

When Yoko won a prize of ten thousand yen for her essay, she not only improved her family's financial situation; she also was able to get some bitter feelings off her chest. Write an essay in which you express strong feelings about a disturbing situation in your own life.

CHAPTER 11

Vocabulary: Use the context to help you determine the meaning of the underlined word in each sentence. Circle the letter of the best definition.

1. The <u>emblem</u> on the woman's jacket showed that she was a government employee.
   a. lint
   b. stitching
   c. buttonhole
   d. badge

1. A good <u>massage</u> may help your aching back.
   a. treating the body by rubbing
   b. soothing the body with lotion
   c. lengthy period of rest
   d. short period of exercise

3. I always prefer a <u>sincere</u> criticism to a phony compliment.
   a. false
   b. candid
   c. abundant
   d. tragic

4. Being an allergic person, the <u>fragrance</u> of any perfume makes me sneeze.
   a. annoying sound
   b. unpleasant aroma
   c. pleasing scent
   d. sweet taste

5. After four months of difficult travel, we looked forward to the return flight and a <u>reunion</u> with our families.
   a. large feast
   b. act of leaving again
   c. act of coming together again
   d. argument

6. Once the river overflowed its banks, it was only a short time until nearby houses would be <u>submerged</u>.
   a. floating on water
   b. sunk below surface of water
   c. damp and musty
   d. demolished

Questions:

1. Why is it risky for the Kim family to hide Hideyo in their home? What is their "cover story" in case he is discovered?
2. Why does Hideyo stay with Mr. Kim and his family until spring?
3. Why does Mr. Kim instruct Hideyo to wear his bag around his hips, rather than on his back?
4. What immediate dangers does Hideyo face when he leaves the Kims' farm?
5. How does Hideyo locate his sisters after his escape from North Korea?

Chapter 11 (cont.)

6. What does Yoko mean when she says, "What's such a big deal about going to see cherry blossoms? I had no space in my heart for such frolicking"?

7. How does Yoko plan to celebrate the fact that she receives straight A's on her report card?

Questions for Discussion:

1. Why do you think the Kim family risked their own lives to help Hideyo?

2. How do you think Yoko and her family were permanently scarred by their war experience?

Writing Activity:

Pretend that you are Yoko, and write a letter to Corporal Matsumura to tell him about Hideyo's arduous journey to freedom, and his arrival in Kyoto.

CLOZE ACTIVITY

The following passage has been taken from Chapter Six. Read it through completely and then fill in each blank with a word that makes sense. Afterwards you may compare your choices with those of the author.

The tracks separated, heading in two directions. Hideyo _____ 1 there. Which way? He looked at _____ 2 sun, which was going down, and _____ 3 the sun as his guide, he _____ 4 the southwest track to Seoul.

As _____ 5 was coming on, the tracks entered _____ 6 narrow gorge through mountains, and Hideyo _____ 7 that he might be able to _____ 8 mushrooms. He had eaten almost nothing _____ 9 he had left his friends two _____ 10 before.

He was not only hungry _____ 11 terribly lonely. To ease his loneliness _____ 12 had thought about Shoichi, Shinzo, and _____ 13 and all the doings he had _____ 14 with them since kindergarten days. He _____ 15 even smiled, remembering some of their _____. 16

He got off the track to _____ 17 for mushrooms and decided to camp _____, 18 for there was no moon and _____ 19 could not see to go on. _____ 20 were plentiful. He stuffed them in _____ 21 pockets of his trousers and shirt _____ 22 the side pockets of his rucksack. _____ 23 he built a small fire. Roasting _____ 24 eating mushrooms, he thought of his _____ 5 and sisters and wondered how they _____ 26 faring – if they were still alive. _____ 27 thought of the bankbook he was _____ 28 and wondered if his mother had _____ 29 money.

He looked up at the _____ 30 sky at the sound of geese, _____ 31 in V formation, heading toward somewhere _____. 32 All talked excitedly as they flew, _____ 33 Hideyo wished he were one of _____. 34 I must hurry, he told himself, I must get to Seoul.

POST-READING ACTIVITIES

1. Write a letter to Yoko Kawashima Watkins, the author of *So Far From the Bamboo Grove*. In your letter, share with her some of your personal responses to her story. Send your letter to her in care of William Morrow and Company, the publisher of the novel.

2. Predict what will happen to Yoko, Ko, and Hideyo after their reunion in Kyoto. What will their lives be like in five years?

3. Work with a cooperative learning group to review the story of Yoko's life. Compile a list of all the acts of kindness people performed in the face of personal tragedy and danger. Compare and discuss your list with lists compiled by other groups.

4. Bring in to class a copy of a newspaper that contains international as well as local news. How many examples can you and your classmates find of instances where ordinary citizens, such as Yoko and her family, have become the victims of government conflicts beyond their control?

5. Make a diorama of a scene from the novel. You may want to create a diorama based on a description of the girls' room in the clog factory warehouse.

6. Have a class discussion to enumerate the personal qualities that allowed Yoko and Ko to survive difficult times. Try to reach consensus on how much of their survival was due to fate and how much was due to self determination.

7. Yoko Kawashima Watkins, who is now an American citizen, did not write this story about her family's ordeal until she was in her fifties. Why do you think she waited so long to tell her story? What do you think motivated her to write her story as a novel for young people, rather than adults?

8. Use a chart such as the one below to compare the journey of Hideyo with that of Yoko and Ko. Write about one event in each box. Whose journey was more difficult?

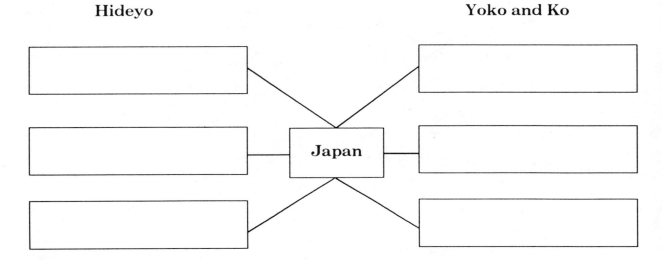

Hideyo   Yoko and Ko

Japan

SUGGESTIONS FOR FURTHER READING

Betancourt, Jeanne. *More Than Meets the Eye.* Dell.

Choi, Sook Nyul. *Year of Impossible Goodbyes.* Houghton Mifflin.

Claypool, Jane. *Hiroshima and Nagasaki.* Franklin Watts.

* Coerr, Eleanor. *Sadako and the Thousand Paper Cranes.* Dell.

Crew, Linda. *Children of the River.* Dell.

DeJong, Meindert. *House of Sixty Fathers.* HarperCollins.

* Fritz, Jean. *Homesick, My Own Story.* Putnam.

_____. *China Homecoming.* Putnam.

Hesse, Karen. *Letters From Rifka.* Henry Holt.

* Houston, James D., and Jeanne Wakatsuki. *Farewell to Manzanar.* Bantam.

Kerr, Judith. *When Hitler Stole Pink Rabbit.* Putnam.

* Levitin, Sonia. *Journey to America.* Simon & Schuster.

* Lowry, Lois. *Number the Stars.* Dell.

* Paterson, Katherine. *Park's Quest.* Dell.

Richter, Hans. *Friedrich.* Penguin.

Wartski, Maureen. *A Boat to Nowhere.* New American Library.

Wiesel, Elie. *Night.* Bantam.

Yep, Laurence. *Dragon's Gate.* HarperCollins.

* _____. *Dragonwings.* HarperCollins.

Some Other Books by Yoko Kawashima Watkins

My Brother, My Sister, and I. Bradbury Press.
Tales From the Bamboo Grove. Bradbury Press.

* NOVEL-TIES Study Guides are available for these titles.

ANSWER KEY

Chapter 1

Vocabulary:
1. d 2. f 3. e 4. a 5. g 6. h 7. c 8. b; 1. emphatic 2. demolished 3. frolic 4. bewildered 5. insecure 6. disfigured 7. vermilion 8. tributary

Questions:
1. Mother and her daughters are planning to leave Korea because Japanese nationals living in Korea are in personal danger as Japan comes closer to defeat. 2. Yoko's family has built shelters and packed emergency supplies of food and clothing as a precaution against the dangers of war. 3. Yoko attacks the policeman. This reveals that she is a fighter who stands up for herself and her family, rather than meekly accepting her fate. 4. Mr. Enomoto tells his students that Tokyo has been bombed and the city almost destroyed. Yoko is not as distressed as some of her classmates because her grandparents live in northern Japan. 5. Corporal Matsumura is grateful to Yoko's family for giving him the will to live by visiting him in the hospital. Their friendship with him proves to be useful when he warns them to escape before the Russian army arrives. 6. Yoko's parents do not support Japan's war policies or the Tojo government. It has destroyed their peace and happiness. 7. Hideyo decides to join the student branch of the Japanese Imperial Army. Ko tries to dissuade her brother by emphasizing his role in the family in case their father is killed and by pointing out that an army that is recruiting the young and wounded is already defeated. It is clear that her plea is effective when Hideyo purposely fails the test and gets a factory job with the army, instead. 8. The women must flee on a train to Seoul because the Russians have landed in North Korea and the family is in danger of being killed.

Chapter 2

Vocabulary:
1. churning – stirring or agitating violently 2. vigorous – strong 3. enveloped – enclosed completely 4. evacuate – to make empty 5. gallantly – bravely, courageously 6. betray – reveal or expose a confidence 7. commotion – state of noise and disorder

Questions:
1. Mother and her daughters almost encounter Korean soldiers who are part of the Communist Anti-Japanese Army. They are drilling ways to kill their enemy, the Japanese. 2. The family is allowed to board the medical train because they have a note from Corporal Matsumura giving them permission. Also, Major Ryu, the army doctor, orders the stationmaster to let them board. 3. Conditions in the boxcar are primitive with very little water and only wooden tubs for toilets. 4. Mother won't allow Yoko to eat any of their food because they do not have enough to go around to the hungry, ailing passengers in the boxcar. Answers to the second part of the question will vary. 5. The medics throw the bodies from the train to prevent disease from spreading. Answers to the second part of the question will vary. 6. Korean Communist soldiers board the train in search of the Kawashima family, a healthy family on board a hospital train. 7. Mother decides that she and her daughters should leave the train because there is a possibility of someone betraying them if they remain.

Chapters 3, 4

Vocabulary:
1. f 2. d 3. a 4. h 5. b 6. g 7. c 8. e; 1. desolation 2. automatically 3. yearned 4. munitions 5. stealthily 6. stench 7. torrents 8. ominous

Questions:
1. As a precaution against capture by the Korean Communists, the women travel by night and sleep by day. 2. On the journey to Seoul, Ko assumes leadership over her mother and sister. She cooks a meal after building a campfire, she scouts ahead to find the road when they get lost, and she manages to safely cross her family over a railroad bridge. 3. Mother, Yoko, and Ko are able to survive the air attack because in air raid drills, they had been trained to throw themselves flat on the ground at the sound of airplanes. 4. The women disguise themselves as Communist soldiers by taking the uniforms of dead Communist soldiers. Mother shaves the girls' heads so they will look like boys and be less vulnerable to attack. 5. Hideyo avoids being killed by smearing

himself with his friend's blood, and pretending that he is dead. 6. Hideyo finds his mother's note because she had placed a rice bowl on top of the sewing machine, which was so unusual that he looked beneath the bowl and found her note. 7. Koreans who are not Communists are refugees because they might be killed by their Communist countrymen.

Chapter 5

Vocabulary:
Across – 2. dehydrate 6. interrogation 7. alumni 8. stout 9. feeble 11. spunky; Down – 1. peril 3. altercation 4. cunning 5. confine 10. asylum

Questions:
1. Ko makes this statement because Yoko has been whining and complaining about everything. Answers to the rest of the question will vary. 2. Mother, Yoko, and Ko have shaved their heads and are wearing the uniforms of dead Korean Communist soldiers. They are mistaken for Koreans by Japanese refugees and Koreans. 3. Mother faints in shock at the checkpoint because she learns that Japan has lost the war and the family will not be able to return to Nanam. 4. The Japanese doctor in Seoul suggests that Yoko must be very brave to endure the pain since she was wounded, as evidenced by her punctured and infected eardrum and her infected body wounds. 5. Mother insists on waiting in Seoul because that is where Hideyo will expect to find them. Ko insists that they get out of Seoul because she has seen Korean men dragging young girls away and raping them. 6. The sisters carve messages for Hideyo on the posts at the train station in Seoul to alert their brother that they are going to Pusan. 7. Ko ties the precious sword to her leg with gauze, and pretends that she is wearing a cast for an injured leg.

Chapters 6, 7

Vocabulary:
1. plunder – objects taken by force, theft, or fraud 2. contagion – a disease-producing agent (such as a virus) 3. mementos – objects that serve to remind 4. endure – remain firm under suffering or misfortune 5. vacancy – empty space 6. compassionate – having a feeling of deep sympathy and sorrow for someone.

Questions:
1. Hideyo does not walk on the tracks because he observes that escapees like himself are being shot from the cliffs above as they follow the tracks to Seoul. 2. As Hideyo tries to get out of sight of the Korean Communist soldiers, he witnesses them taking plunder from those they have ambushed and killed, and he even sees one Korean soldier shoot his companion to get a greater share of the loot. 3. Hideyo keeps up his courage with thoughts of being reunited with his family. 4. Yoko is disappointed because she had always dreamed of her beautiful homeland and she is now faced with the reality of a war-torn country. 5. Mother knows that Kyoto is one of the few cities in Japan that escaped massive bombing in the war, and that there will be an opportunity there for the girls to get an education. 6. Mother tells Yoko that she is going to school to learn and become an educated person; there is no reason to decorate herself. 7. Because Yoko has suffered such privation, she unashamedly scavenges scrap paper and pencils that she will need. She is also able to withstand the cruelty of the girls who ridicule her.

Chapter 8

Vocabulary:
1. d 2. c 3. e 4. b 5. a; 1. tatami 2. anguish 3. crematorium 4. urn 5. prestigious

Questions:
1. Yoko befriends the trash man because he saves scrap paper and other school supplies for her. She also has compassion for his stuttering and believes she can help. Also, Yoko is lonely because the other students avoid or ridicule her. 2. The trash man rips up the drawing because it makes fun of Yoko's habit of collecting scrap paper from the trash. He adamantly defends his friend, not wanting her to be hurt by the cruel girls. 3. Yoko suddenly feels protective of Mother because she notices that Mother is pale, very tired, and seems to be breathing with great difficulty. Also, Mother has just given Yoko the news that all of their grandparents were killed in the war, and she is crying. 4. Yoko expresses bitterness when a Buddhist monk refuses to say a prayer for Mother and slams the temple door in the girls' faces. 5. The sisters make an altar for Mother using the mess-kit urn filled with her ashes.

Chapter 9

Vocabulary:
Questions:

1. earnestly 2. negotiating 3. staggered 4. vicinity 5. humble 6. reverently
1. Mother's last words, "Hang on to the wrapping cloth," haunt Yoko because she feels there must be some special significance to the contents of the wrapping cloth. The girls soon discover a secret pocket filled with money. 2. The sisters travel to Maizuru to try to locate Hideyo since Maizuru has become the new port for refugees arriving from Korea. 3. On New Year's Eve, Yoko discovers that Ko has set up a shoeshine business near the Kitano shrine in order to make extra money. She feels guilty because she has been resenting Ko's bossy attitude. As reparation for her ill thoughts and attitude, Yoko spends her shoe money to buy traditional New Year's foods for her sister. 4. In Japan, everyone gains a year, not on the date of his or her birth, but at the New Year. 5. Yoko and Ko's relationship has become stronger and they respect each other to a greater degree. At the start of their journey Yoko resented Ko.

Chapter 10

Vocabulary:

Questions:

1. d 2. g 3. f 4. a 5. b 6. e 7. c; 1. wracked 2. textile 3. spared 4. snobbish 5. numb 6. suspension 7. prohibited
1. Ko amazes her classmates by revealing her excellent skill, that of sewing a white silk-lined kimono with colored thread without the thread showing. 2. Even though they have a place to live, winter is very hard for Yoko and Ko. Yoko's shoes are threadbare and since most people are wearing boots in the winter, Ko's shoeshine business suffers. Yoko is unable to find bottles and cans to sell for extra money. 3. Yoko's essay, "Understanding," criticizes the snobbish behavior of her classmates, who have *not* been understanding at all. Yoko saves her prize money for food. 4. The school was displeased with Yoko's essay because it was critical of the students at the school. In Japan it is very rude to bring shame on the members of your group. 5. Yoko does not reveal her mother's death because she is afraid that she will be expelled if the school authorities discover she no longer has an established guardian. 6. Yoko's reunion with Corporal Matsumura brings back memories of her life in Nanam before she was forced to flee. Also, his presence reinforces the fact that Father and Hideyo are still missing.

Chapter 11

Vocabulary:
Questions:

1. d 2. a 3. b 4. c 5. c 6. b
1. It is risky for the Kim family to hide Hideyo because all Japanese refugees are now criminals in North Korea, and they could be executed for hiding him. Their "cover story" is to tell the authorities that Hideyo is Mr. Kim's nephew. 2. Hideyo stays with Mr. Kim and his family because he needs to recuperate and because any suspected Japanese will be killed by Korean Communists. 3. Hideyo wears his bag around his hips in order to appear more like a Korean, since it is the custom for Koreans to carry bags around their hips. 4. Hideyo must travel four miles South in perilous North Korean territory before he reaches the relative safety of the region south of the 38th parallel. He must cross a wide river with a strong current that is under heavy surveillance by Korean Communist soldiers. 5. Hideyo locates his sister's whereabouts when he arrives in Maizuru and finds their hand-printed signs. 6. Yoko means that she cannot enjoy the cherry blossoms because she has too many cares and worries: her missing father and brother, her lack of tuition, her constant concern about food, etc. 7. Yoko plans to celebrate by buying two tea bags for herself and Ko.